For Girls Like You! Coloring Book

TEXT BY WYNTER PITTS
ARTWORK BY JULIA RYAN

HARVEST HOUSE PUBLISHERS
EUGENE, OREGON

Illustrations and cover design by Julia Ryan | DesignByJulia.com

For Girls Like You Coloring Book
Text copyright © 2020 by Jonathan Pitts
Artwork copyright © 2020 Julia Ryan | DesignByJulia.com
Published by Harvest House Publishers
Eugene, Oregon 97408
www.harvesthousepublishers.com

ISBN 978-0-7369-7961-0 (pbk.)

Printed in the United States of America

20 21 22 23 24 25 26 27 28 / VP-RD / 10 9 8 7 6 5 4 3 2

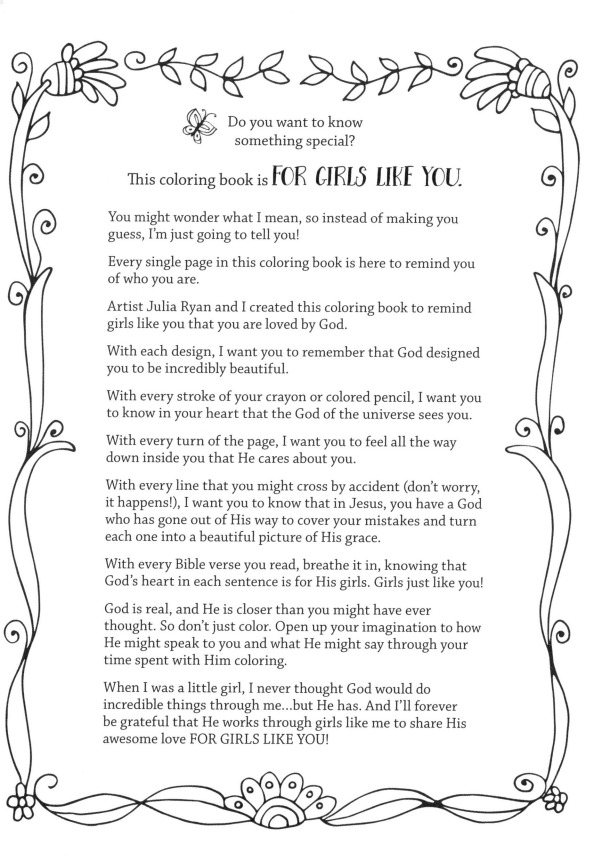

Do you want to know something special?

This coloring book is FOR GIRLS LIKE YOU.

You might wonder what I mean, so instead of making you guess, I'm just going to tell you!

Every single page in this coloring book is here to remind you of who you are.

Artist Julia Ryan and I created this coloring book to remind girls like you that you are loved by God.

With each design, I want you to remember that God designed you to be incredibly beautiful.

With every stroke of your crayon or colored pencil, I want you to know in your heart that the God of the universe sees you.

With every turn of the page, I want you to feel all the way down inside you that He cares about you.

With every line that you might cross by accident (don't worry, it happens!), I want you to know that in Jesus, you have a God who has gone out of His way to cover your mistakes and turn each one into a beautiful picture of His grace.

With every Bible verse you read, breathe it in, knowing that God's heart in each sentence is for His girls. Girls just like you!

God is real, and He is closer than you might have ever thought. So don't just color. Open up your imagination to how He might speak to you and what He might say through your time spent with Him coloring.

When I was a little girl, I never thought God would do incredible things through me...but He has. And I'll forever be grateful that He works through girls like me to share His awesome love FOR GIRLS LIKE YOU!

Fill your heart AND mind with drops of God's love.

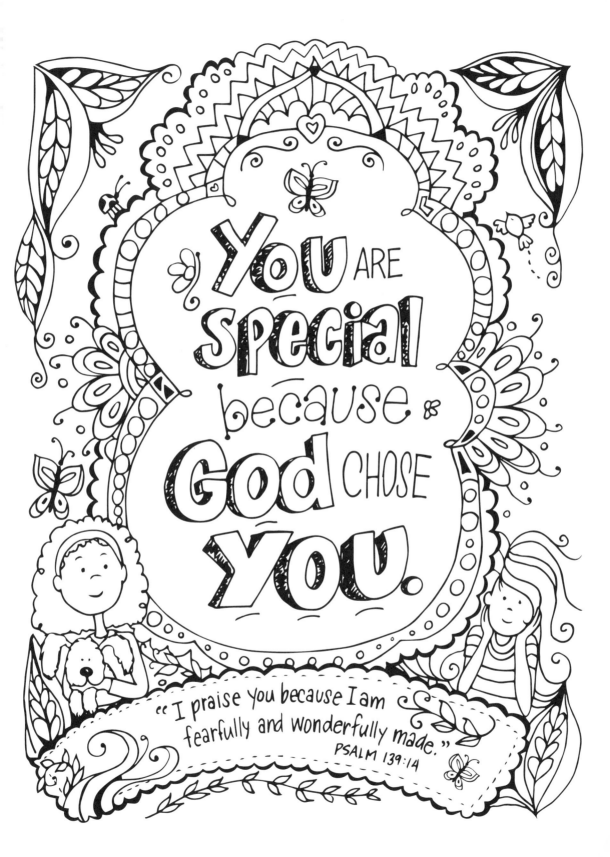

YOU ARE SPECIAL because GOD CHOSE YOU.

"I praise you because I am fearfully and wonderfully made." PSALM 139:14

"WHATEVER is true...
WHATEVER is lovely...
WHATEVER is admirable
~ if anything is excellent or praiseworthy ~
think about such things." – PHILIPPIANS 4:8

SHOW JESUS with your WORDS, attitudes, AND actions.

READING

BAKING

PAINTING

CLICK

WOOF

MEOW

MUSIC

HIKING

"Whatever you do, work at it with all your heart."

COLOSSIANS 3:23

Sweet LIKE Honey

"Gracious words are a honeycomb,
sweet to the soul and healing to the bones."

PROVERBS 16:24

"Where your treasure is, there your heart will be also." Matthew 6:21

Brighten someone's day.

"Create in me a pure heart, O God, and renew a steadfast spirit within me." PSALM 51:10

GOD IS OMNIPRESENT.

°°° HE IS WITH ME ALL THE TIME. °°°

"Devote yourselves to prayer, being watchful AND thankful."

COLOSSIANS 4:2

WYNTER PITTS is the author of several books, including *You're God's Girl!* She is the founder of *For Girls Like You*, a bimonthly magazine that equips girls to walk boldly into who God has created them to be and to resource their parents to raise strong Christ-following God girls who say yes to His plans for their lives. Wynter tragically passed from death to life on July 24, 2018, after 15 years of marriage to her beloved Jonathan. She leaves behind an incredible legacy through her many writings but more importantly in her four daughters—Alena, Kaitlyn, Camryn, and Olivia.

JULIA RYAN has enjoyed a long and successful career as a graphic design professional and accomplished artist. Her diverse clientele includes the National Geographic Society and many Christian publishers. Julia lives and creates in the beautiful mountains of Colorado with her husband, Kerry, and their endless list of property improvement and garden projects.

To learn more about Harvest House books and
to read sample chapters, visit our website:
www.harvesthousepublishers.com